Adesua's Big Adventure

Learning About Money

By:

Leasia Ezeogu

Illustration by: Tejal Mistry

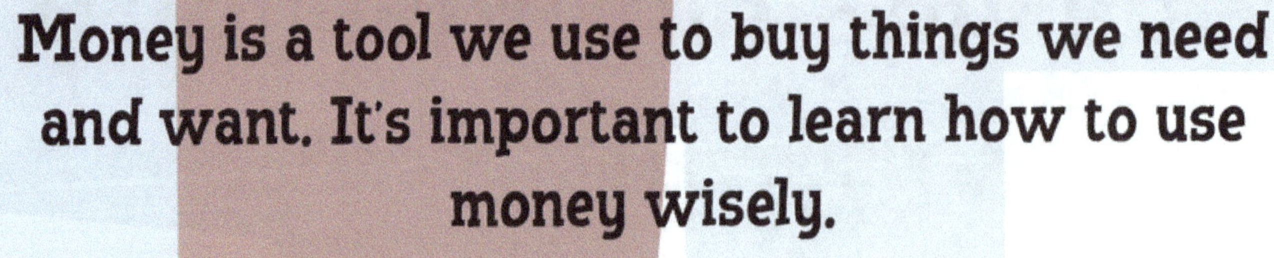

Money is a tool we use to buy things we need and want. It's important to learn how to use money wisely.

INVOICE
PAY
TAX

Meet Adesua. She's a curious girl with big questions about money. One sunny day, Adesua's parents gave her a small allowance. Adesua wondered, 'What can I do with my money?'

Adesua's mom said, 'You can earn more money by helping with chores.' So Adesua washed the dishes, cleaned her room, and helped in the garden. With each chore, she earned a few dollars.

"Great job, Adesua!
Here's $23 for your
hard work"

With her saved money, Adesua bought a stuffed giraffe. She felt proud of her purchase and understood the value of saving.

Adesua's dad gave her a piggy bank. 'This is for saving,' he said. 'When you save your dollars, you can buy something special later.' Adesua smiled and dropped her dollars into the piggy bank.

"Saving money helps us buy bigger things we want in the future."

One day, Adesua went to the store with her mom. She saw a beautiful doll she wanted to buy. The storekeeper explained, 'You can buy this doll, but remember, you have to choose wisely because your money is limited.

"Do I want the doll more than anything else right now?"

Adesua noticed her friend Ellie was sad because she didn't have enough money to buy a book she wanted. Adesua decided to share some of her dollars with her. 'Here, Ellie. You can have some of my money,' she said.

"Thank you, Adesua!
You are so kind,"

Adesua wanted to earn more money, so she decided to set up a lemonade stand. She worked hard and earned even more dollars.

That evening, Adesua's parents taught her how to make a simple budget. They gave her three jars labeled 'Save,' 'Spend,' and 'Share.' Adesua divided her money into the jars, making sure to put a little in each one.

"This way, you can always have money for what you need and want,"
SHARE

Adesua felt proud of all the things she had learned about money. She shared her knowledge with her friends, teaching them how to earn, save, spend, and share their money wisely. 'Learning about money is fun and important!' Adesua exclaimed.

"Now we know how to be smart with our money, just like Adesua!"
SPEND
SHARE

Every evening, Adesua pretended to be a news reporter. She stood in front of her mirror with a toy microphone and talked about everything she learned about money that day.

"Good evening, everyone! Today I learned that saving money can help me buy bigger things in the future,"

color me!

Match the coins to their values

Draw a line to match each coin with its value

One Cent

five Cents

Ten Cents

Twenty
five Cents

fifty Cents

Draw something you want to save for

Draw something you want to save for